i just want freedom

i just want freedom

b. binaohan

biyuti publishing
Toronto

dedication

this is for you

and you

but not you

Contents

prologomena

a somewhat random collection

of what might be called

'philosophical prose poems'

or maybe

'anti-oppressive un-sonnets'

or it could be

an ode to hate

acknowledgements

i'd like to formally and explicitly thank two of my biggest influences re: writing:

- Bad-dominicana @bad-domininincana
- BlackAmazon @Blackamazon

i wish i had the words to express how much your writing moves me

s
how much it has transformed me and worked on my spirit

i thank you both

to the kind patrons of biyuti publishing

this is a very hearty "thank you" to Cecily Walker, Johannes Wilson, and two anon people, for contributing to make biyuti publishing a sustainable project.

this would literally be impossible without you.

so thank you.

for supporting my publisher (and indirectly me)

u r magnificent human beings

1

and really

if you are white your opinion on racism and
its history is generally not needed

but when you add your bullshit white
mythology onto a post talking about

how other white people are trying to co-opt
and steal my ID

and that is what you are quibbling with?

gtfo

2

one of my forever rage buttons is ppl acting like begging for money and receiving it is contingent on some level of ~worthiness~

fuck you.

ppl need to fucking eat. to pay rent. buy clothes. get manicures. get some chocolate. maybe go see a movie. or a concert.

i don't fucking care.

3

one of the axioms i live by:

the oppressed are who name their
oppressors

4

How to be an Ally: Don't Oppress Me!

5

any serious vision of the future as free, absolutely must account for vulnerable populations and have solid plans to protect them.

6

Thing I resent white trans/gender theory for:

Telling me I have a 'medical condition'

Isn't there some way to make your point without legitimizing the medical industrial complex?

I kinda feel like you've failed to make your point that trans women are women if you make any references to biology. It isn't relevant.

My gender isn't a disease cured by medical transition.

And if *your* gender is, maybe stop acting as if your experience is universal.

7

Not really.

because i do understand who the audience is
(not me)

but i also understand the harm that
educational posts like yours

do to people like me

for all the ways that it erases, exploits, and
appropriates

me and my gender

your post isn't 'weak' because it reifies and
centres the white, male experience

indeed, this is your post's strength, since it is
the job of white men to ensure that they and
their experiences are seen as the only viable
and real ones

in that, your post is massively successful

and we have nothing to talk about.

8

And seriously

I don't care about how the galaxy works.

Don't fucking care.

I want resources and shit going to solving our problems here.

9

I'm not joking when I say that my hero of the moment is Balpreet Kaur.

I would be happy to even have an ounce of her grace.

I'm inspired.

And reading her response to the reddit shit

was just the balm I needed

for all the dysphoria I've been feeling lately

10

clear sign that people want you dead:

thinking that $30 spent on food is too much

11

With the notion to also confuse white people with our 'not a fucking monolith'

i want to say that for me

when i say white people i do mean the institution

but i also mean every single individual white person

all of you

are like that

12

fyi

ur super feminist point stops being meaningful

when you casually use transmisogynist terms

in making it.

jsyk

13

every time the whole historical accuracy thing comes up and it is "oh there were no poc anywhere near my precious movie"

when will whites learn that poc where everywhere.

all the time

and they should just get the fuck over it already

14

Seriously. White people are the only people i know who create communities out of doing nothing.

Beards.
Atheism.
Breathing.

15

at this point

that i've come to recognize a red flag in ppl's theorizing about
anti-oppression

i see so many people

who when talking about oppression

coincidentally accidentally just so happens

manage to always and continuously frame oppression

such that they are always

the 'most' oppressed

and thus

the judge and jury of whose experiences are valid, who isn't conscious
enough, who is 'in' and who is 'out'

nowadays

if i see elements of this in ppl's writing

i just walk away

16

ugh. so annoyed. i saw the word 'dick panties' before seeing the giant transmisogynist shitpile it is and, for a moment, was like really hopeful. I mean. i would like panties designed for girls with junk. it would actually be really, really useful. but… nope! silly, biyuti, dick panties and queer friendly and challenging gender whatever the fuck isn't for #girlslikeus

17

right?

we started this conversation. the movement. everything.

but. hey.

i'm apparently standing in the way of white cis women and/or white trans people.

or something.

18

but really

any discussion about why gay men hate
femmes and stuff

that doesn't involve race and transmisogyny

is a waste of time

19

I'm also suspicious enough to think that one of the reasons

why white mainstream feminism does very little about radfems is **because** they benefit from their actions.

it strikes me a lot like handwaving and misdirection.

the more focus and energy we spend engaging radfems

only serves to distract us from what the rest of white feminism is doing

because they are no more for #girlslikeus than radfems

20

dreams of the day ppl will stop making proscriptive and normative claims about gender like they are facts

21

ugh.

i just want… girlslikeus to be free to be ourselves

without having to worry about be rendered unhuman and degendered because
we don't meet up with transmisogynist and racist requirements

i want

fuck it

i just want freedom

22

white expat communities are predicated on never integrating into the cultures and lands where they are squatting

integration and participation in the local economies would mean that their subjective experience of wealth would be similar to whatever they were at back home.

and they only go to those countries **because** they are able to exploit the poverty, fetishize the culture, etc.

they support and enforce white supremacy because (as it does at home) it benefits them

and it benefits them in direct, material, and tangible ways.

which is why they **love** doing this so fucking much.

23

some white cis d0Od
(*cough*theylooklikebigstronghands*cough*)

on that post about Lucy Meadows

arguing about free speech and how we'll
never stop people from posting hate speech

go away.

step on a lego

don't fucking talk about how best to 'honour'
Lucy Meadows or any other trans woman

go fuck yourself

24

hahhahahahahaahahah

What a fucking joke. Is this what history shows us? Show me just *one* group that has won its freedom with facts, 'reasoned' arguments, thoughtful ideas, and loud debates. Just one.

I've said it a million times:

Fuck white reason

Fuck white science

and fuck all the white liberals who think this is the path to freedom.

25

And of course

This is what damage the medicalisation and pathologizing of trans women has done

The silence of the lambs represents what many cis people think what trans women are like

And not even in some hyperbolic way. They literally think that we are James gumb.

Especially a certain group of mostly white cis women.

26

omg. this is why counter-factuals and/or subjunctives are so dangerous.

“if he was the killer, then these people would have knowledge”

what.

that is very very poor fucking reasoning.

if you apply modus tollens, then if the people have no knowledge, he wasn’t the killer.

i don’t think it works like that, buddy.

27

okay. i need to go to bed and stop laughing at that post.

wormholes! geography! evolution!

zomg. white people are like, seriously, the most smartest and beautiful and bestest of all the races.

like…

almost godlike in their abilities.

28

"the space between people and ideas"

this space is an illusion

it is the space where accountability goes to die

29

like

the level of white feminist discourse i encounter most days

seriously is still at the stage of

uncritically discussing 'female' representation....

which, again,

is kinda amusing since, i swear to fucking god,

hasn't it been generally accepted in mainstream white feminism

that 'biology isn't destiny'

that biological essentialism isn't actually a thing?

and

still

still

‘female characters’

‘male privilege’

interesting how white feminism appears to
be all about reifying and supporting
ideologies they claim to support…

30

i'm amazed

that ppl seriously think that 'innocent until proven guilty'

has any viable meaning or application outside of the courts

like

the entire catholic religion is founded on 'guilty until proven innocent' vis a vis ~original sin~

In turn

much of white morality (since much of it is influenced by christianity) also follows this principle

even if not....

this is like the millionth time some clever person has decided to point this out

except...

i don't care?

i don't have to buy into a major principle of
one of the most morally bankrupt
institutions of us/canada settler states?

lol.

just. lol.

31

i have zero interest in lowering myself to be equal with white people

freedom is the name of the game

32

Fuck this shit.

I'm gonna take a wild guess and say this is a cis white gay man?

Fuck you and your 'seperatist movements' shit.

Fuck you for trying to appeal for the common good in a movement where you and people like you have systematically worked to not only exclude tpoc but have consistently *erased* the contributions that twoc have made.

IN conclusion, fuck you.

33

you've pretty much already failed

the moment you run a women's centre

and starting thinking about how to make the safe spacer

for non-women

before you make it safe for all women

34

interestingly,

it'd be interesting to see aces actually realize that this movement they seek inclusion into, is problematic as fuck

and they'd probably be much better of starting their own shit and doing it right, instead of unquestioningly accepting the current systems designed to exclude/oppress twoc.

like, you are looking for a path of freedom in the wrong place. (well, okay, if your also white and cis, you'll probably get some measure of freedom by reifying the bullshit politics of the lgbt movement)

35

I swear, everytime I see the word 'anchor babies' I wanna punch a white person in the throat.

The shit the white community comes up with never fails to shock me with how utterly disgusting it is.

36

And look

It is white people who use 'science' as a way to claim eminence in knowledge creation and innovation.

It is but one method and not necessarily the best method.

One just needs to look at all the awesome shit people did before there was white science.

(And it is white people who frame science as a white invention. This is why we constantly get all these white people saying 'if you hate white people so much, you should give up your iPod!!!11!!')

37

how ppl are seriously trying to assert that white supremacy hasn't crept

into pretty much all aspects of history for a large portion of the past

500 years

esp. when talking about genocide....

which is a word invented to literally describe something that white people do

and one of the things they taught to the world

38

i cannot understand

how so many science evangalists do not seem to get how

the fact that science isn't neutral, that it is falsifiable

that it can change, be challenged

is one of the absolutely *best* things about it

39

And, really, at the end of it all.

If the PoC manner of using 'gay' had won the day (instead of the white cis version)

trans/gender variant poc would have a shitton more rights and protections than they currently do

instead we have to fight for distinct recognition, something that is proving both tough and very costly

(how many lives are lost?)

40

That random moment...

when a colonial practice that removed many of the cultural contexts for getting tattoos

gets valourized because of how

white middle class people

appropriated tattoos from

lower class white people

who appropriated it from

IaoPoC people the world over

who practiced tattooing as means to express community ties, prestige, spiritual connections, coming of age, etc. etc.

41

was just thinking (before i go to bed)

about how much better my life has been since making definite boundaries for how i engage ppl

like

not debating my humanity with ppl?

seriously a fucking awesome decision

my life is way more peaceful

42

I mean…

there is a reason why so many white academics on tumblr/the world act like they are entitled to every fucking thing.

it started when they first saw PoC and started cataloguing, writing, committing to paper everything thier narrow and creepy light eyes could see

i mean

none of us are human, right?

43

to make other things clear:

i don't like the trans movment.

i don't like the queer/gay/lesbian/etc. movement.

i don't like the atheist movement

i don't like the kind movment.

the poly movement.

hmmm....

thinking it over.

also don't like the disability movement.

the fat acceptance movement.

i don't like **movements**

i don't belong to any. don't want to belong to any. don't believe in any.

44

i seriously hate it

when white europeans pull this shit

'in eruopoe, the spanish/italians/greek/
whatever the fuck aren't
considered white...'

orly?

italy? had colonies in Africa. forever and
always they are white white
white.

greece is certainly having no problems
identifying who isn't white enough
to stay in there crountry *right now*

honest to god

i know very well that white imperial
america has done *a lot* of evil

but they are not the 'worst'

and they didn't invent all of this by
themselves

45

it is also telling that the person linked

critical thought to logic

as if there is some inherent relationship
there

this is another lie taught by whiteness

46

1. Race is always relevant.
Especially for white people.
2. Because white women have a long history of treating woc bodies as subhuman.
3. Because the woman was white.
4. And that matters.
5. It always matters.

Also annecdote.

This week I encountered two cis women who were both strangers.

One was a cis Black woman.

One was a cis white woman.

Draw your own conclusions.

47

trying to understand the logic

of someone with, apparently, no need to
tuck

going onto a post for tucking and other
skills

asking about what a certain tip does

why are you asking this?

why do you think you need to know?

why do you care?

this isn't for you. you don't need to know
what #girlslikeus are doing
with our genitals. or not doing.

go away.

48

Lol,

no.

did the ~patriarchy~ tell white feminists to be so racist?

or cis feminists to be transmisogynist?

or middle class/upper class feminists to be classist?

this kind of one-dimensional anti-intersectional thinking is not a problem created by the patriarchy

but good job trying to dodge accountability in this way

E- for effort

49

i've said this things before

but here they are again

I WILL NOT DEBATE PEOPLE'S HUMANITY

AND

I DO NOT PLAY RESPECATIBILITY
POLITICS

don't care if you think i'm rude

don't fucking care

i care about all the people you clearly cannot
see as human

50

@ that pro-injustice warrior

"if they hadn't blocked me, which suggest
they are a sjw"

okay.

i didn't realize i was obliged to engage every
white tool with no grasp of history

apparently they've decided to focus on
reblogging my old posts now

gud job

and i'm having to see comments from other
white ppl with that terrible

disease that afflicts so many white: willful
ignorance,
subtype: selective reading

51

any theory that fundamentally states that
Black americans can never be free is

anti-Black

linguistic determinism/relativism
essentially states this

it is also faintly ridiculous to assert this

while at the very same time

so much of Black american culture

is constantly co-opted and exploited

by non-Black ppl

in our own struggles for resistance and
liberation

52

fuck

this is why history is such a critical thing

and not the white mythologies

but like actual history

people seirously think that white supremacy started in the US

really

really really?

white people in north america

inherited the white supremacy they got from spanish, english, and french.

this is why i fucking hate the way that people talk about europe as this super progress awesome place

and decry us-centrism, even as they blame the US for shit they did

53

be very careful who you give your history to.

your history is fucking *precious*

54

I find this debate about lady gaga's bisexuality bizarre.

and pretty pointless.

she says she's bi, she's bi.

being bi doesn't excuse how she has exploited gay men.

doesn't excuse her ongoing ableism.

doesn't excuse her transmisogyny and transphobia.

doesn't excuse her racism.

she remains and continues to be a shitty human being.

all while being bi.

55

i wish there was a way

To really and truly show my appreciation for all the people on tumblr who've done so much to inspire me, touch me, encourage me, make me feel less alone, and generally give me so much life.

All these people who are so generous with their experiences, their thoughts, their feelings, and give so much of themselves.

A way to really show that I like them best when they are being shy, awkward, ebullient, kind, thoughtful, excited, playful, etc. ... because it means so much that they can be these things with all the shit, horror, ignorance, terror, dehumanizing crap that I see them wade through on a daily basis.

I would give a lot just to be like five and pushing them on the swings or having an ice cream cone or doing some other frivolously fun activity where it'd be nothing but giggling and laughing.

57

i'll have you know that white middle class
teen girls are a dime a dozen

but one Black trans girl is priceless

so. no. they don't have equal value.

:P

58

The interesting thing to me.

About saying that ppl have a responsibility to educate....

Is that some ppl who actually decide that this *is* how they want to spend some of their time are, at turns,

1. Outright ignored, like no one will talk to them. This happened with me for a long time. I know it happens to others.

2. Expected to set no boundaries or rules for engagement. Like, you have to be available 24/7 and can't, say, expect ppl to engage go good faith.

3. Subject to abuse when ppl don't have a super fun time getting their education. This isn't kindergarten, if you don't think learning is fun, that is your problem.

There is a reason many of us end up giving up on doing it at all. It is exhausting, thankless, and often futile.

59

if you r white and adopt poc babies

and this is what you need to finally, at long last, see poc as fucking human beings?

you suck.

and you shouldn't be allowed to have those babies.

60

anyone who hasn't actually tried to live off
of minimum wage should probably

stay out of conversations related to how

minimum wage =/= liveable wage

61

perhaps the time has come

to politely ask

all white people to never talk about
Stonewall again. ever.

unless you were there, kindly shut the fuck
up.

even when you try to get it right. you still get
it wrong.

if you talk about Stonewall without
explicitly mentioning

- race
- trans women (of colour)

u r doing it wrong and should shut the fuck
up forever

62

white queers not making history

no one's fault but their own

no one made you love brunch, white
supremacy, and capitalism

more than freedom

63

one of my favourite things about
decolonization

is being taught to see beauty in people i was
taught were ugly

(this includes myself)

64

one of my least favourite things about
oppression

isn't that it treats you as worthless

but that it convinces you that it is deserved

65

it is important to remember that white people conquered the world

only by being more violent, vicious, and monstrous than anyone thought was possible

they stay in charge because we, in many ways, still cannot fucking process what they are capable of, even as they continue to do it[1]

is the moment i've lost myself

1. this is also why i think working within white power structures corrupts so thoroughly. they are meant to debase you and strip your humanity. because i think the moment that you truly — in your heart and spirit — understand why white people do as they do, you're lost. which is why it is not necessary to understand white people, or seek the motivations for their actions. because, the moment that settler colonialism, chattel slavery, genocide, etc. become comprehensible to me, the moment that i can rationally understand this,

66

on signs of abuse

so i'm seeing that go around. and all the people making points that sometimes these signs are useless because understanding your situation is abusive doesn't do much if you lack the resources/support/ability to extricate yourself from the situation.

something that always strikes me about it

is that these lists don't really address the fact that, for some of us, these abusive relationships started with our parents.

who, unfortunately, we were entirely dependent on for many years.

and who socialized us to believe that these kinds of relationships are normal

so once we get out into the world

those bullet points aren't 'signs of abuse' but 'qualities we are looking for in relationships'

so that maybe you look for someone
controlling because that means they love
you

that maybe you look for someone who
crosses boundaries you didn't even know
you were allowed to have

that maybe you can only trust that person
who puts you down all the time because
they are the only one being honest with you
(all those people who say you are great and
deserve better are just fucking liars)

worse too, is that abuse culture is such that
we are continuously exposed to media and
narratives that actually confirm that abusive
relationships are what we should want
(twilight, anyone?)

so you make a list: these are the signs of
abuse

when really, i'm looking for a partner/
friend/lover/etc with those qualities.

how else will i know that i'm loved?

67

i think the thing with microagressions

is that they are like water

slowly and inexorably

eroding

your confidence

sense of self

you

68

since some have forgotten

how this whole oppression thing actually works

the default for white people is racist

the default for cis people is transmisogynist

the default for men is sexist

the default for able people is ableist

I'm sure you are seeing the pattern by now

these defaults are what happen when you grow up in a society with institutional oppression. the are literally unavoidable.

we must all unlearn these things

(the difference between people who experience an oppression vs. those who do not experience it is the target: self or other.)

do not now or ever again ask for proof that a
white person is racist.

you want me to think they aren't racist?

show me the proof that they are anti-racist

69

It is never a discussion or debate when your central thesis/point is that I (or someone else) is not human.

My humanity is not up for discussion. Neither are my experiences nor my identity.

I do not engage people who don't get this. I may give a quick reply or comment, but the next thing I do is always to block the person.

Repeating

My humanity isn't up for discussion.

Supplementary list of things also not up for discussion:

Facts. Lived experience.

70

can u srsly not c the dif. b/w being a monster
2 ur kid and being a monster 4 ur kid?

71

it boggles my mind

how many people seem to not get that one of the operations of power and oppression is erasing its tracks just enough so that the people benefiting don't have to be aware of their privilege.

that is seriously one of the major aspects of privilege: the privilege not to know (to be ignorant)

because as far as you're concerned, everything is working exactly as it should

there is nothing wrong.

(and, note, the 'erasing' of the tracks is often just the normalization of oppression such that these things are happening in plain sight, but people think it is okay)

72

this is why i never try to use teh word
'patriarchy' when i write

ppl mistake my writing for feminism

no, sir, madam,

i do not do teh *F*eminism

okay?

73

i feel like there is this… idk, sort of competition for people to appear more jaded/blasé than everyone else when it comes to the supreme shittiness of what oppressors will do.

but, i think, the problem with this.

is that at some point we will all be shocked. not because of privilege or having our heads in the sand

but because part of how we got to this place, is because on a very fundamental level, we will never comprehend just how far and how much (white/cis/hetero) people will do to maintain their power

because however low we think they can go, they always go lower.

74

it is always important to remember that the academy

has turned ‘knowledge’ into a commodity

it occurs within a capitalist system

designed to exploit, oppress,

if u just want to ‘learn’ about another culture/place/people

y not just read wikipedia?

save your thousands of dollars

buy a book. whatever.

75

just saw a white person mention 'binarism'

and. yeah.

we've talked about this before:

if you are white, regardless of how non-
binary your ID might be, you
actually benefit from binarism

because 'binarism' as a thing is, at heart, a
colonial (and frequently
transmisogynist — in so many cases) tool

used by white people

to surpress and eliminate people like me

and TWoC

and, for that matter, what you'd call 'binary'
cis poc.

remember white ppl who invoke binarism

remember why it is a thing. and who
benefits

76

but. since i’ve been negative all evening.

what do i believe in?

I believe in us. people. but especially the oppressed. we’ve been resisting for so long. and we are still here. and i believe in our desire to be free overcoming all who oppress us.

i believe we’ll all get there. i don’t know how. but i have faith that we will.

this is the faith and love that keeps me going.

77

It is amusing to me that the best evidence someone can find of my dire reverse racism is tagging pics of white people as 'mayo'

like.

hahahahaa

unlike you, I have 500 years of colonization, genocide, eugenics, occupation, settlement, etc. etc. violence death subjugation

this is my (our) evidence

(also, you would *rather* a Black man get hit than a white woman or white baby? of this I have no doubt and this is exactly why I TW violence against Black people. It is *necessary*)

78

Don't talk to me about community responsibility, you sack of shit

does it make me feel better and like CAMH could be more accessible knowing that a white d0Od had a better time navigating its transmisogynist and white supremacist labyrinth of shit?

not at all

i don't have a responsibility to whatever community you belong to

we are not in the same community

your community (the white trans d0Od community) can go fuck itself

79

This notion that the greatness of iaopoc is reducible or created from whiteness is disgusting and plain wrong.

80

ppfem disgust with our bodies is literally what feeds their moral judgements about trans women. and why they cannot let it go to focus on something productive. we disgust them and must not be allowed to live

81

r ppl srsly this confused about gender-based oppression?????

men aren't harmed by the patriarchy

BECAUSE THEY ARE THE PATRIARCHY

they are not victims here

each of them make the decision every single day to oppress women

just as all white people are actively choosing to be racist every second that they aren't being anti-racist

we do not need our oppressor's participation to get free

literal actual human beings are the components and parts of the systems/ institutions of oppression

it doesn't harm 'everyone'

it harms the oppressed

and benefits the oppressor

82

but.

like everytime white people get all mad
about one of my tattoo posts

and call me stupid, uneducated, etc

but.

it literally takes **one** google search

to verify whether or not what i'm saying has
any historical basis in fact.

one. google. search.

but. some are too lazy and arrogant

to ever think that my mouth can speak the
truth

83

of all the kinds of whiteness and white
people i loath and hate

the spanish will always

be no. 1 on my list

always.

because

because

i'm

pilipina

84

but really that

concern troll logic

(omg. this sounds like that buffy line.... you know, with olaf? hahahahaha)

anyway. concern troll logic says

"Look. i see that you are tired and fed up with being subhuman, may i suggest you just accept it?"

hint:

I WILL NOT ACCEPT IT

i will continue to cherish my

hate

bitterness

anger

and revel and wallow in my glorious humanity

85

the only full proof way to avoid being
robbed or sexual assault

is

for ppl not to do those things

so

stop, okay?

86

do white ppl ever get sad that they are so bad at history?

lol.

omg. this person.

“white ppl have had/used third gender since the mid 19th century, so it is
not racist for us to use it”

mid 19th century? this is what you are going with?

it isn’t like transmisogyny and the pathologization of gender

started with colonial encounters with 3rd gender iaopoc

not at all

and not like colonization hasn’t been ongoing for over 500 years.

but hey, 60 years ago some crackers started using 3rd gender/sex

and clearly i owe my identity to
feminists of all ppl

or white queers.

87

lol

white woman's tears never fail.

No one was bullying you

Unlike what you encouraged people to do to me.

And how does that empathy fail work?

"I don't like being bullied, but send hate mail here"

You know…

I hesitated for a minute because I saw that you are young.

But you are an adult. Old enough to be held accountable for your decision and actions.

Only a white woman would interpret accountability as being bullying.

You fail as a human being.

88

sometimes i truly believe

that white people are allergic to history and context.

but maybe the reason why we have to stay good at history is because we have to keep it all in our heads

even when we write our histories down, they are buried under the piles of white lies and misinterpretations

or filtered through the white gaze

but history is what grounds us

history, for us, is a form of resistence.

and white people hate us

because we never forget

89

so i'm still listening to these lectures on
sociology 101 on iTunesU
given by a prof at nyu.

for the most part, what I'm understanding
sociology to be:

the white academic discipline responsible
for co-opting and consuming

liberatory discourse

and regurgitating it pre-chewed, mushy,
faintly disgusting bite-sized
chunks for other people in power.

about 99.99999% of their insights appear to
be summed up as

"we could have just *asked* marginalized
group x, but instead we spent
tons of time and money learning what a five
year old from group x
already knows"

90

I want to be weak. To be allowed to fall apart.

To be a human being. Not just this…

Surviving waking nightmare.

91

"justify trans men as natural enemies of trans women"

no.....

there isn't anything 'natural' about trans men setting themselves up as the enemies of trans women (fuck, other women too).

it is almost like you think being trans means that men are no longer men and women no longer women, and thus trans men are magically not oppressing trans women, despite it being fairly well evident that cis men oppress cis women.

'defame trans men'

LOL

omg.

it is almost like you are saying that us understanding that trans men are.... drum roll please... *men* and understanding that, as men, they oppress us, as women. is like.

defametory and, idk, something that needs
to be established.

it isn't defamation if it is *true*

92

I just saw that 'let us make awesome pictures
with menstral blood in
public restrooms'

this is so fucking disgusting.

for years i'd have been the sort of person
who cleaned something like that
up (having working in cafes for 10+ years)

like.

really.

you think smearing around your
biohazardous waste is *feminism*

i'm so grossed out right now

93

it is never a good idea

to ask someone with a heavier burden

to carry you and yours

94

since most (middle class+) discussions about budgeting while poor

almost never ever

include any mention of debt

no mention of utility debt (ie, not paying your bills)

no mention of credit debt (for that credit card you got before your credit was ruined)

no mention of student loan debt (b/c you bought into the american dream that college = awesome fucking job)

no mention of the money you owe friends/ family kind enough to get you out of a tight spot

95

i care

and i don't care that i care

i wallow in my caring

fucking bathe in it.

96

any critique of capitalism that does not include race and gender at its core is shit

ugh. and that person saying that critiques of the state as being racist or sexist is shallow.

particularly on the race front

if you cannot fucking get how our current system of capitalism fundamentally rests on the exploitation of poc labour

how your notions of 'future capitalism that isn't racist' is ridiculous

because capitalism requires white supremacy to function.

or not understanding how resisting and dismantling white supremacy fundamentally means economic justice

yet.

it is our/my analyses that are shallow and not-real

hmm hmm

97

once my mom told me that she wished she never had me. she stopped saying this after i said i wished she hadn't either.

98

Yup. When people talk about things being 'only language' as if language weren't one of the most important repositories of a people's history, identity, and collective self.

I always wonder about those people who think language is irrelevant. Then again it is pretty clear that they have the luxury of never feeling that special pain that a lose of language has (or at least a complicated relationship).

And for those of us who have lost our languages… transforming, reclaiming, redefining is really the only true strategy we have for resisting linguistic colonization.

99

rhetorical questions for white ppl:

For those deeply and truly concerned about being anti-racist and checking their shit…

How prepared and comfortable are you with the notion that even if you do everything right, some PoC/non-white/Indigenous people will never trust, like, or love you? That some may always hate your whiteness and all the privilege that comes with it?

Are you prepared to not travel to non-white countries if there isn't a good, ethical way to do so?

Are you prepared to stop doing yoga, stop getting tattoos and other body mods, etc.?

If you are doing area studies of non-white ares (i.e., Asian studies, etc.) are you prepared to change your major? Career?

Are you really able and willing to accept that some spaces will never be for you and that you are unwelcome there?

I wonder… (but seriously, these question are rhetorical)

100

it almsot makes me feel pity

that white feminists

after all this time

still have a position that essentially boils down to

“i’m the most oppressed ever!!!”

while standing on the backs of woc

this all that they’ve managed to contribute

to a long running discourse on gender-based oppression

jsut this.

they build their empires of dust and shit

and are just so

sad….

about the author

b. binaohan

is a transpinay ladyboy

she likes manatees

because they have button eyes

and are so soft and squishy looking

appendix a

Now. The standard reasons apply so I won't say too much about them.

(standard reasons: white people feel entitled to everything, don't seem to know how to history, can't figure out either context or nuance, don't recognize anyone's boundaries but their own, hate being told anything, etc. etc. etc.)

Tattooing is such an integral part to white north american counter-culture. And so what we get are not necessarily the people who are racist or white supremacist is more overt ways, but people who often pride themselves on being better than other white people. People who are heavily invested in this notion of resisting the dominant white culture.

These people aren't necessarily political (I mean, a lot of the body mod community is just this sad community created off of being alternative or whatever and their shared privilege of being able to afford expensive body mods and very little else). But some of the people are. Some of the hordes of people in the white community getting tattoos or other body mods (particularly stretching) are those who are political. Who maybe even identify as radical and thus push white exceptionalism into this realm where they feel better and superior to other white community members.

And just when they are feeling smug and maybe complacent, some jerk like me makes a post asking them to consider the origins of the contemporary western tattoo and how it is inextricably linked to colonialism and suddenly they are realising that they may have been unconsciously participating in a questionable activity. And this questionable activity cannot be taken back because, for most people who get them, tattoos are permanent. So maybe the must defend what they did and why they did it because otherwise they may have to accept that they have visible and permanent marker of their privilege.

This happens like every time I say *anything* about tattoos even though I always and repeatedly say that is essentially pointless to try and get people to stop. And how it is a far more useful approach to simply encourage people not to get appropriative images or styles. Like… I fucking get it. nothing can actually be done about white people getting tattoos. And I don't actually want to do anything about it because I have better things to do with my time than try and ineffectually challenge a billion dollar industry when I have no resources and certainly not enough time.

Instead, all I've been asking is for white people to think about their privilege and the history of tattooing and understand how their actions do occur within a larger colonial context that they need to be aware of. And not even about just tattoos because this is shit that they should be thinking about anyway (or at least the good ones do).

Like. I just want them to think about what it means for them to spend thousands of dollars to seem counter-culture when poc people (particularly Black people) usually cannot get tattoos without people thinking they are criminals. Or how in places with Indigenous tattoo traditions, like say the Maori, are having to fight to retain their practices without stigma (especially with facial tattoos). Or how like in the Philippines the tattooing tradition mostly has died out *because* of white people and their bullshit colonial religions. How white people do this as a nominal act of rebellion while in my culture tattoos were about affirming your place and status in your community. How the act of a white person getting a tattoo has many different layers of meaning but they are still privileged because poc just can't get them for the same reasons. And even when poc do want to get them, some will be turned away, some will be harassed, many will have to grit their teeth not through pain but through a 1000 different microaggressions, how they'll have to pay a white tattooist to get something that might be part of their own cultural tradition but they can't do it that way because white people killed that tradition (or nearly killed it or maybe the person doesn't know who their people are as a result of colonialism or maybe they don't have the same connection with their home culture and maybe it is just fucking complicated).

But no. You are too busy getting sailor tattoos without realizing what it even means that sailor tattoos were a thing. How sailors and their tattoos and all the 'nostalgic' shit going along with it represents the beginning of american imperialism and shit. how during this period of awesome sailor tattoos america was occupying the Philippines and other Pacific Islands and their sailors were getting tattoos as a way of marking their complicity with this.

However. It appears too much to ask the white community to reflect on this stuff and maybe to some of their own heavy lifting to actually think about their actions beyond their fierce individualism and the "I can do whatever I want without consequences" bullshit they so often reply with.

because. Yeah. You can do whatever you want. And if you think that I don't realize that this (and other posts by other people) is basically futile because you'll just continue on doing whatever you want... you'd be mistaken. If you also think i write this to try and convince individuals to do anything, you are also mistaken. If you think that I believe that change is only possible via changing the minds of those who oppress me... you have zero idea what I'm actually about.

Made in the USA
Middletown, DE
25 January 2019